I was Minding My Own Business

My Spiritual Autobiography

Doctor/Pastor Daisy May

To order additional copies of this book, contact:
stevenspresspublicationsllc.com
702) 508-6837 | (702) 508-6824 | (702) 508-6835

Not being spiritual or anything else, God interrupted me when I was trying to get rich and famous in the entertainment business. He asked me to choose, and I believe I made the correct choice.

Dedication

This autobiography is dedicated to my Father, my God, my Lord Jesus Christ, and to the Holy Spirit. In His mercy, He chose to show me that Jesus was real and not a Steven Spielberg fantasy. This little book is also dedicated to everyone who reads it: Avril Vavrosky, who years ago tried to get me to put my story in a book, but I was too lazy and thought that it would be boring; Bonnie Shumate, the queen of the universe who helped me with the title; the Schlossins, Rick and Mary; Barbara J. Layton, whom if I had not met in Bethel, it would have been a very nonadventurous life; Pastors Jacob Rock, Michael Pilla, Ricke Schlossin, Matt Hinton, and Johnny and Sue Ellen Shoemaker, Laurel Franz, and Ron and Rose Peters; the New Hope Church Family; the Jesus in the City Family;

Women of faith who have helped me change me, and everyone else I may have forgotten—this is not the Academy Awards; your reward will be in heaven.

I was minding my own business... Who are you?

You want me to do what?

The wonderful thing about writing your own biography is that you can reveal anything you want about yourself. With that in mind, I will be transparent while also making sure that Scripture and God are in the forefront. I love Him with all my heart, mind, and soul. We can talk all we want about making a difference in the world and making it a better place, impressing our mark on the world, or having a legacy, which, I guess, is all right; but unless our core objective relates to ways in which we serve people to the best of our abilities, it's all just talk. When you love and serve others like Jesus did, the impact of your service keeps rippling out further and further, affecting more people than you will ever know.

I have learned an awesome truth: little acts of kindness and love have a ripple effect. Serving and preaching the gospel unconditionally opens up many opportunities to do even more acts of service and reach greater numbers of people with God's redemption and love. I have come to the conclusion that the will of God is to remove His anger upon human beings and replace it with His kindness, mercy, and love. This can only be done by the good news in the New Testament. Without the ministry of evangelism or being a speaker/PR person for God, the other ministries would not stand. The message is the good news that God has acted, for the salvation and restoration of the world is in the incarnation, death, and resurrection of Jesus Christ of Nazareth. The Bible is the good news of hope, immortality, peace, and sanity. The blind can receive sight, the mute can speak, cripples can walk, cancers get healed, people are raised from the dead, young people see Jesus, and AIDS and HIV get healed. He can and has done all these, and with me, He healed me from hating myself.

I want to make myself clear. Evangelism, speaking for God as an ambassador, is the mode by which nations are changed, cultures get impacted, and the world is transformed. Every church that hopes to win souls for Christ must put evangelism at the forefront. The power of evangelism is not rooted in great education, for how can you master the divine? ("When you receive your Master of Divinity degree?" or oratorical ability.) Not everyone is TD Jakes, with untold wealth and riches, fame, or deep understanding of the scriptures. As much as all these things are important, the power of evangelism is rooted in the Holy Spirit. Words alone cannot bring a soul to salvation and gesture of kindness is not enough. These things are needed, but to be effective, they must be accompanied by the Holy Spirit. The Holy Spirit draws people to Himself; we are not God, and if we are honest with ourselves, not everyone wants to be saved. However, evangelism that is inspired by the Holy Spirit of God brings a permanent transformation of lives, nations, and generations.

The evangelism in which I was called to do communicates the good news and becomes a catalyst of God's message. Humanity in our spiritual state is dead and has been separated from God. He is under a curse because of wickedness and immorality, and he is an enemy of God. However, thank goodness, God offers reconciliation and regeneration. From the beginning of time, when God

2

created the heavens and the earth and established the universe, when He gave breath to human beings and caused them to live, He has always sought a way to communicate His desire to us. He has always desired to have communication with us, but sin has frustrated God's desire.The Bible teaches the theme of redemption from Genesis to Revelation. Throughout the Bible, one can see the plan of God to rescue humanity from its "fallen from grace" state. That plan was revealed clearly by the words of Jesus in Matthew 28:18-20, in what has become known to the modern church as the Great Commission. This is a commission to evangelize to the world. It is a mandate to communicate the will of God to men and women.

In an effort to restore human beings back to their original state, God chooses evangelism as the mode of communication. On the bus, in the store, on the street, at work, on the plane, at church (not everyone is saved in the pew), at the conference, at the park, walking the dog or cat, riding the bike. He commissions all believers to go and communicate the good news of Jesus. The good news alone gives life. It is like taking breaths there's no alternative. Free will gives us the right to make choices, but it doesn't give us the power to create them. Just as breathing air is the only option for natural life, believing the good news is the only option for eternal life. We die if we don't breathe, and we die forever if we don't say we are sorry to God for our sins. God's Holy Spirit is the hand that fits perfectly into the glove of the preached Word, Jesus Christ. At the creation that I mentioned earlier, the Spirit was hovering over the chaotic waters awaiting the Word. When God spoke the Word, the Spirit began to act.

It is the same today. When God's gospel is preached, the Holy Spirit storms like Thor into action. Our thinking should be as Romans 1:16 says, "I am not ashamed of the gospel of Christ, for it is the power of God to salvation for everyone who believes." God made Himself real to me in a very special way. I did not go to heaven or died, but after what He did to me, I felt like I did died, that is. I went to a Jimmy Swaggart Crusade, granted this was before the scandal with him and later Rev. Jim Bakker. My roommates at the time said that it would be wonderful. They never said it had nothing to do with partying, or I would never have gone. Being the social butterfly that I was, I thought I would be dancing, dancing, and dancing besides having rum and Coke. When I arrived at the stadium and saw all these people happy before anything was happening, I thought to myself, *this is weird, and how are we going to party with all of these people?* To make a very long story short, seeing all of these people raising their hands and speaking in tongues, as well as the country fla-vored music had me thinking that I was either in a cult or in hell or both.

Needless to say, I wanted to get out of there as fast as my little feet could take me, but there were too many people, and I had no idea where the bus stop was to leave. I was thinking, what did I do to deserve this when Mr. Swaggart started preaching on John 3:16, 17, 18 and started waving something that I found out later was a King James Bible. Now I have never seen a Bible in my life, and I always thought it was a shame that a man was on a cross, but I never knew the story and had no idea it, or rather He was and is God who was hung up there. I felt a wooing in

4

my being and ran up there to get saved like everybody else. I was crying and happy, my roommates were crying and happy, and I was told the angels were partying because of me, which at the time I thought was interesting to know.

After three months when you love Jesus, you should too wore off, I thought to myself, which I am beginning to realize is a dangerous thing, that maybe this was just mushy, mushy rah-rah stuff that made me go up. I had really missed partying and I was beginning to wonder if this was an emotional rather than a rational decision I had made. That was when a group of Christian friends of mine said that they were going to a Bible study group and asked if I didn't mind to come along. Well, I decided that if I was going to continue with this Jesus thing, I should at least have an idea how to read and understand this Bible because when I got to Leviticus, I was lost and the talking snake had me confused. I mean, how can a snake talk and then have the audacity to walk upright? Much later on, I discovered through science that a long time ago, snakes could stand up and for some reason that can't. Fascinating. Anyway, I decided to go with the gang and get some knowledge.

I was in a Bible Study group in the military with a stoic Asian gentleman leading the group. We had just read Acts 2:38 in the New Testament. After the gentleman read the Word and talked with everyone, he asked me if I believed that the chapter he had read was real. I told him basically that I believe the Bible from Genesis to the Maps, and that I just needed to reassure myself that this wasn't just emotional for me but that this Jesus was real then and real now and not just a legend. He was going to pray for me, I thought, then someone, I mean something, He, the Holy Spirit (God), picked me up and knocked me down on the floor. I didn't feel a thing, like hitting a pillow with a hundred volt of electricity hitting me, and I had a very, very close encounter with the Holy Spirit of God, who is part of the Trinity. There is God the Father, God the Son, and God the Holy Spirit, and I had a close encounter with God the Holy Spirit. Until this experience, I didn't even know that God will do almost anything to get your attention. Just for the record, I didn't even know that He existed, even if at times I wished He did.

Let's see I laughed, cried, felt a hundred volts of electricity throughout my body, felt drunk and I knew how being drunk is, since I was in the Navy but I digressed, couldn't move, was down on the floor for approximately thirty to forty-five minutes, speaking in a language I don't understand (I apologize to my strongly Baptist people). I thought I was going to go straight to heaven if this feeling didn't stop, but finally it did, and I got converted. I should also explain that a few of my friends went down along with me. I bring this up because my friend, whom I shall call Mr. P., was already a believer Presbyterian, I believe and he never raises his hand or, for that matter, gets emotional. Mr. P. was on the floor shouting and raising his hands in the air like a maniac and feeling good and going "Hallelujah in the highest!" Scary. It did not stop there either; there was a nice sweet Southern Baptist dude, whom I shall call Bubba Bubba, and he thought all this was nonsense and that he was going to pick up this skinny at least at the time I was Black girl from the floor and straighten everything out. There was a problem: he couldn't get me off the floor, and believe me, he was trying. That was when I realized this is really happening and this Holy Spirit, who was God, still does things that get your attention. I don't know what happened to the Southern Baptist young man, but all I remember was poor Mr. P. shouting with his hands in the air, driving like he was drunk well, in a way, he was and so was I. I haven't felt that good without cocktails, anyway, since I joined the Navy, and this was pure hundred percent God.

I was wondering how I was going to go to work in the morning and explain why I was feeling good and shaking all over. I could see it now, I thought, Hi, I am not drunk. I just had a nice encounter with God, thank you very much, and everything would be all right. Fortunately, it didn't come down to that; the feeling and encounter went down to a human minimum. Most Christians today understand Jesus the Son and God the Father as two very distinct Persons within the Godhead; however, there has been much confusion over the identity of the Holy Spirit. Perhaps some of this dates back to the King James Translations of the Holy Bible where the word spirit or ghost was used instead of breath or wind of God. In any case, many people throughout the ages have thought of the Holy Spirit more as a thing than a Person. Nothing could be further from the truth, and in fact, as we begin to know the Person of the Holy Spirit, we will want to have a closer relationship with Him just as we would the Father or Son. Although the word trinity is not mentioned in the Bible, we know God is three in one. The Holy Spirit of God was way on the scene long before the day of Pentecost and way before I had a close encounter with Him. He moved upon the face of the waters and was the active agent in creation. Jesus was the Word, and the Holy Spirit moved.

In the beginning God created the heaven and the earth. Genesis 1:2 And the earth was without form, and void; and darkness was upon the face of the deep. And the Spirit of God moved upon the face of the waters. Genesis 1:27 So God created man in his own image, in the image of God created he him; male and female created he them. The Holy Spirit gave us the Word of God. 2 Peter 1:20-21 Knowing this first that no prophecy of the scripture is of any private interpretation. For the prophecy came not in old time by the will of man: but holy men of God spake as they were moved by the Holy Ghost. The Holy Spirit regenerates our spirit when we accept Jesus Christ into our life. John 3:6 That which is born of the flesh is flesh; and that which is born of the Spirit is spirit. This is what I found out about the Trinity, especially the Holy Spirit: 1.The Holy Spirit is God, but He is a Person, not a force like in Star wars. 2.We cannot focus on the Holy Spirit too much. Why? What is the Holy Spirit's mission? To reveal Jesus Christ of Nazareth. What is Jesus mission... to reveal the Father. What about the Father... to send Jesus and the Holy Spirit so we can come to Him. 3.The Holy Spirit gives gifts for use in ministry and empowers effective ministry. 4.The Holy Spirit is a distinct Person within the Godhead, not a force, like I have said before a thing, or an "It." The difference between a force and a person: 1.The Holy Spirit has intellect. 1 Corinthians 2:10 says But God hath revealed them unto us by his Spirit: for the Spirit searcheth all things, yea, the deep things of God 2.The Holy Spirit has knowledge. 1 Corinthians 2:11 even so the things of God knoweth no man, but the Spirit of God. 3.The Holy Spirit has emotions. Ephesians 4:30 And grieve; to make sad or sorrowful, heavy of heart, not the holy Spirit of God, whereby ye are sealed unto the day of redemption. 4.The Holy Spirit has his own will and he makes decisions. Acts 16:6 Now when they had gone throughout Phrygia and the region of Galatia, and were forbidden of the Holy Ghost to preach the word in Asia, 5.The Holy Spirit loves, Romans 15:30 Now I beseech you, brethren, for the Lord Jesus Christ's sake, and for the love of the Spirit, that ye strive together with me in your prayers to God for me; They (The Father, Son and Holy Spirit) are all: Omnipotent All powerful. Luke 1:35 And the angel answered and said unto her the Holy Spirit shall come unto you, and the power of the Highest shall overshadow you: therefore also the holy thing which shall be born of you shall be called the Son of God. Omnipresent At all places at once. Psalms 139.7 Where shall I go from your Spirit? Or where shall I flee from your presence? Omniscient All knowing. 1 Corinthians 2:10 But God has revealed them unto us by his Spirit: for the Spirit searches all things, yea, the deep things of God. Eternal Hebrews 9:14 How much more shall the blood of Christ, who through the eternal Spirit offered himself without spot to God, purge your conscience from dead works to serve the living God? Equal-Acts 5:3-4 But Peter said, Ananias, why has Satan filled your heart to lie to the Holy Spirit, and keep backpart of the price of the land? While it remained was it not your own? And after it was sold, was it not in your own power? Why have you conceived this thing in your heart? You have not lied unto men, but unto God. The Holy Spirit always worked hand in hand with Jesus His Birth-Matthew 1:20 but while he thought on these things, behold, the angel of the Lord appeared unto him in a dream, saying, Joseph, thou son of David, fear not to take unto thee Mary they wife: for that which is conceived in her is of the Holy Ghost. Ministry Luke 4:1 And Jesus being full of the Holy Ghost returned from Jordan, and was led by the Spirit into the wilderness And... Luke 4:18 The Spirit of the Lord is upon me, because he hath anointed me to preach the gospel to the poor; he hath sent me to heal the brokenhearted, to preach deliverance to the captives, and recovering of sight to the blind, to set at liberty them that are bruised. Jesus death a sacrifice, Hebrews 9:14 How much more shall the blood of Christ, who through the eternal Spirit offered himself without spot to God, purge your conscience from dead works to serve the living God? Resurrection of Christ Actually all 3 members of the Godhead had a part in the resurrection. Father-Ephesians 1:19-20 And what is the exceeding greatness of his power toward us who believe, according to the working of his mighty power, which he wrought in Christ, when he raised him from the dead, and set him at his own right hand in heavenly places. Son-(He had the power to take His own life up again)-John 10:18 No man taketh it from me, but I lay it down myself. I have power to lay it down, and I have power to take it again. This commandment have I received of my Father. Holy Spirit-Romans 1:4 And declared to be the Son of God with power, according to the Spirit of holiness, by the resurrection from the dead; In fact, the main purpose of the Holy Spirit is to tell us about Jesus and glorify Him. John 16:13-

14 Howbeit when he, the Spirit of truth, is come, he will guide you into all truth: for he shall not speak of himself; but whatsoever he shall hear, that shall he speak: and he will shew you things to come. He shall glorify me: for he shall receive of mine, and shall shew it unto you.

What I experienced was what happened on the Day of Pentecost where Jesus said it was imperative that He went or that the Spirit not be sent. Jesus felt it important enough for them to wait until the Spirit came to empower them. Jesus's own mother needed the baptism of the Holy Spirit to be an effective witness. On the day of Pentecost, the believers who were assembled in the Upper Room experienced a new baptism, the one which John the Baptist (no pun intended) referred to. There are many scriptural references that show the co-existence of the entities within the Trinity.

Luke 3:22 And the Holy Ghost descended in a bodily shape like a dove upon him, and a voice came from heaven, which said, Thou art my beloved Son; in thee I am well pleased. Here we see the evidence of the Father, Son, and Holy Ghost all mentioned within one verse. We also see the same reference elsewhere in the New Testament. Matthew 3:16-17 And Jesus, when he was baptized, went up straightway out of the water: and, lo, the heavens were opened unto hi, and he saw the Spirit of God Descending like a dove, and lighting upon him: And lo a voice from heaven, saying This is my beloved Son, in whom I am well pleased. Mark 1:10-13 And straightway coming out of the water, he saw the heavens opened, and the Spirit like a dove descending upon him: And there came a voice from heaven, saying, thou art my beloved Son, in whom I am well pleased. And immediately the Spirit driveth him into the wilderness. And he was there in the wilderness forty days, tempted of Satan; and was with the wild beasts; and the angels ministered unto him. Things only a Person would do (Not the Force) 1. He teaches you things about God and yourself. John 14:26 But the Comforter, which is the Holy Ghost, whom the Father will send in my name, he shall teach you all things, and bring all things to your remembrance, whatsoever I have said unto you. 2. He tells the truth. John 15:26 But when the Comforter is come, whom I will send unto you from the Father, even the Spirit of truth, which proceedeth from the Father, he shall testify of me: 3. He guides. John 16:13 Howbeit when he, the Spirit of truth, is come, he will guide you into all truth: for he shall not speak of himself; but whatsoever he shall hear, that shall he speak: and he will shew you things to come. 4. He convinces. John 16:8 and when he is come, he will reprove the world of sin, and of righteousness, and of judgment: 5. He prays for you. Romans 8:26-27 Likewise the Spirit also helpeth our infirmities: for we know not what we should pray for us as we ought: but the Spirit Himself maketh intercession for us with groanings which cannot be uttered. And he that searcheth the hearts knoweth what is the mind of the Spirit, because he maketh intercession for the saints according to the will of God. 6. He commands. Acts 13:2 As they ministered to the Lord, and fasted, the Holy Ghost said, Separate me Barnabas and Saul for the work whereunto I have called them. This brings me to my story, and why I wrote this small book. My goal if anything is to make God famous in a more positive way and not negative as it has been. It says in 1 Peter 3:15, NIV Version instead of King James, "Always be prepared to give an answer to everyone who asks you to give the reason for the hope that you have"

When was the last time someone asked you to give a reason for the hope you have, why you love the way you do, or why you're so sympathetic, compassionate, and, I hope, humble? I don't know about you, but I am getting this a lot. And if I am reading 1 Peter 3 correctly, it sure seems like a chunk of this chapter is telling me to be ready to respond, how to communicate in the midst of tsunami, earthquakes, suffering, and evil. I went to a women's conference and was kicked literally in the pants to tell what God has done for me and to share it with whoever asks me. The Holy Spirit Him again took ahold of me with no one realizing it, basically letting me know that a wild ride is coming if I say yes to God and preach the gospel. I had not had a shaking in my spirit like this since the Hawaii experience, and I want you two or three people who are reading this to know that this whole book is about God, from the front to the back, and that it is not about me. The title of this book is true because I was only minding my business happily, going to eternal doom, when the God of the universe had mercy and grace and took a low-life, crooked, fornicating, lying, partying, greedy, and self-centered woman and changed her perspective throughout the years. Anyway, going back to the knockdown of the Holy Spirit, I ministered to anything human that had legs. After researching and realizing finally whom I was dealing with, I got the CCM anointing and I went everywhere there was a hint of a conference or concert. From that experience,

I went to every Christian concert I could get to, like Carmen, Sweet Comfort Band, BJ Thomas, even Pat Boone. I bought a copy of the Bible for each translation and talked my mother into getting Jesus in her life over the phone. Let me begin this by saying that after too many years and too many people telling me that I should write a book after hearing my story, this is it. It's dedicated to my God, family, friends, and enemies thank you very much.

I was born in Brooklyn, New York the year is not important at the moment, but let's just see, Nixon wasn't president yet. I lived mostly in my early age in the South Bronx, where rival gang members of rats and roaches invaded constantly where I lived. (They never made peace among themselves.) My mother was not well, and I don't mean physically; I meant in the head. When your mother is taking you to X-rated movies and saying to you rather seriously that they have their clothes on when you know that they don't and she is happy with that, well to put it nicely, Mother was nuts. She loved me, thoughat least most of the time she did allow me to eat first whenever we were able to find food. Let me also mention that physical and verbal abuse was going on for years to the point where I thought this happened to every normal family. Actually, I found out that being normal is just a setting on a washing machine. The fact that I enjoy and love God and have a nice, sweet husband and friends and even enemies who love me, life was not always so easy. I have since forgiven my mother, who died in 1989; I had to, God wanted me to. Oh, I failed to mention that I was an only child and that my father died when I was three years old. Here is my unedited, uncensored story of how God getting into my business prevented me from being a star.

I had plans of becoming an actress and winning the Tony Awards, the Grammys, the Oscars, and the Emmys; the only problem with this is that I had no talent whatsoever. I gone to the Actor's Studio, where Marilyn Monroe, Marlon Brando, and others went to study what they call the method acting and did a little off Broadway in New York City. I even auditioned to get into Brooklyn College in their Theater Department and got in. Happy Days was popular at the time, so I used one-liners that the Fonz used, such as "Sit on it" to the other actor who was playing a boring Casanova who wanted to impress me. Then there was also an audition for a new taped version of a new show that was coming on television, which was called Saturday Night Live. The actors on the show were John Belushi, Jane Curtain, Chevy Chase, and two others one of them an African-American male, the only one. I believe the guest host was Steve Martin, who was then an unknown at the time. Anyway, there was an audition for a taped version of the show. During the time, I was going to Brooklyn College as a Theater Major and I saw a posting for females to audition. Streaking was popular at the time, although I was not going to streak. Let me explain I was one of, I believe, ten women who were left to see if we could make the cut. The actor who was with the director was chasing the women behind the table and making pretend he was streaking them. When it came to be my turn, the only Black female in the bunch to be chased, I turned the tables on him and chased after him. Before I caught up to him, I was told that I was hired. I believe that taped film of us doing the streaker incident in Brooklyn at Carvel ice cream parlor never made it to the show, but it was nice and cool doing it. I do wonder, though, whatever happened to the film.

Since I did not want to end up on the couch, sleeping with people to get a part, I joined the Navy instead. I did not have to audition; however, I did discover later on since doing ministry that my calling should have been as a stand-up comedian. Oh well, it is what it is; I do it for God now. In 1983, when I was twenty-six or twenty-seven years old, I was stationed at Pearl Harbor Naval Base in Hawaii. One night, my roommates invited me to a crusade. Hearing it was a crusade, I thought I was going partying, which I did with all of my might. I had never seen a Bible before and didn't know who Jesus was except as a cuss word. But that night, I heard the good news of God, and it launched me into a lifetime of service for Jesus. Now you wouldn't expect someone with no interest in ministry, no desire to attend seminary (I thought that was what nuns did), and no inclination to live in Minnesota to be pursuing a master of divinity degree at Bethel Theological Seminary in Arden Hills. But I discovered with God to expect the good and downright ugly.

I had later received my BA, graduating as cum laude in Mass Communications from Benedict College in Columbia, South Carolina. I had no interest in ministry whatsoever and was only thinking about graduate school. My idea of ministry was to get rich so I could give to the poor, but every Frank, Dick, and Mary was telling me that I was called into the ministry of evangelism. Bethel was the first to accept me, but I really was not interested because of cold, snowy fortress inhabited by masses of smiling cold White and Black Lutherans. I wanted to suffer in sunny California or at least Hawaii. I came to Minnesota crying and weeping with God practically grabbing my ankles and dropping me off. To make the story short, I went to various church internships, got licensed in full gospel Baptist Church, and got ordained in a Baptist General Conference Church, and in both cases minding my own business. Also, in one women's conference I attended, I was minding my business, sitting down and looking at my Bible, when I accidentally looked up, and the pastor pointed at me and said I was one of the speakers. Fortunately, God showed up at the meeting, and I was saved. He still does that with me.

Just recently, I went to a Women of Faith Conference for free. Yes, free hotel, airfare, transportation, food; it was wonderful, and I realized that God was serious in having me talk about Him. I can never repay Bethel for the wonderful professors who trained me, Dr. David Clark, Professor Ralph Hammond, Dr. Robert RakeStraw, Professor Herb Klem, Dr. Donald Verseput, and Pastor Anne Waters, who taught Black preaching. All of them showed me how to incorporate what I learned in the classroom, to bring out the good news to the people who need it. Sometimes it is weird to look back on one's life and see how God has pushed or pulled it in different directions. Growing up in a rat and roach infested ghetto, I would have never guessed that I would one day emerge from seminary to where I am now. In fact, if someone would have told me years ago that I would become a speaker or evangelist, I would have asked them, "What kind of drugs are you taking because it is not working for you." I know I am right where He wants me to be. I would never have planned this. But we must never forget where we came from or what God brought us out of. By the way, Bethel College and Seminary did not pay me for including them in this biography. If I had bad things to say about the seminary, it would not have been put in. I have met some nice people while attending there Bonnie, Barbara, Mike the Cat, Pastor Michael, Wendy, and people whose last names I won't use just in case they decide to sue me for using last names. Just kidding, they know I have no money; I am not yet on Christian Television. All I am saying is this: never tell God what you are not going to do. You will one way or another find yourself doing what you said you wouldn't.

Somehow people enjoy God's use of me talking about Him. That in itself is a miracle because I used to believe that I was boring to people. But when you are talking about the God who shows compassion and love to good, bad, and especially ugly people, I found out He will listen to you. I had recently gone to a Women of Faith Conference in Las Vegas. I had never been to Vegas before, and all I knew about Vegas is from watching Elvis Presley's movies with Ann Margaret, singing "Viva Las Vegas." The trip was free all way round free food, hotel, transportation, and airfare and I was, like, God, why are you sending me to Vegas? I knew it was not to gamble and see the Strip.

John 3:16-17 is what got me into Jesus's love for me. Jesus and Holy Spirit of God, thank you for not leaving me when I was acting the fool. I have been low on hope and feeling rejected, a bit diva, and far from you. You allowed me to come as I am, just as the song goes, and it was really ugly. Thank you for letting me come to you for real this time, without the theatrical mask I used wear to hide the real me. As I did that, even before you changed my circumstances, you began to change my mind, heart, and spirit. You are an awesome God, and I feel unworthy to even consider writing about how you saved me from myself so I can show your light to others. I wish that I could hold you and kiss you right now. The Word is His love letter, and He is the best thing that can happen to anybody. Blessings.

About the Author

Doctor/Pastor Daisy May was a former chaplain in the army, Individual Ready Reserve (IRR). Originally from Brooklyn, New York, she moved on to live in Minnesota, where she became the pastor of Heights Church senior group online ministry and volunteer staff chaplain for MNTC in Minneapolis. She is currently pursuing a Doctor of Divinity degree, which she expects to finish by spring 2022.